— THE MAKING OF A —
Cowboy
DOCTOR

—THE MAKING OF A—
Cowboy
DOCTOR

KYLE VER STEEG MD

LitPrime
"Your story is our priority"

LitPrime Solutions
21250 Hawthorne Blvd
Suite 500, Torrance, CA 90503
www.litprime.com
Phone: 1 (209) 788-3500

Published by LitPrime Solutions   12/12/2020

ISBN: 978-1-953397-54-6(sc)
ISBN: 978-1-953397-53-9(hc)
ISBN: 978-1-953397-55-3(e)

To my wife and soul mate, Phyllis. Without her love for nursing and tireless help in our doctor's office, my career would have suffered and this book would have never been written.

CONTENTS

INTRODUCTION

This is a true story about a doctor who, as a young man, developed a fierce independence. His goals became not only to become the best doctor he could be but to be his own boss.

It's also the story of a healthcare system that became hostile to that independence, such that to continue as an independent doctor became riskier over time.

This is my story. I'm that doctor who, at times, had to risk it all just to be my own boss.

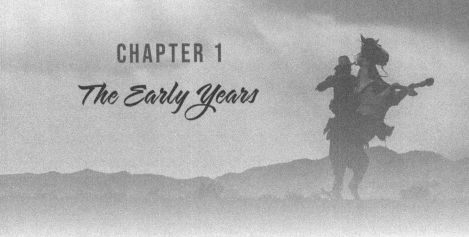

CHAPTER 1
The Early Years

I was born in 1946. My "white privilege" was growing up in a two-parent family with traditional middle-class values. These values became instilled before I was even aware of it. I was the first son of a college athlete and a high school football, basketball, wrestling, and baseball coach. He reportedly once told his football players that he had a bad dream about me marching in the band rather than playing football. As it turned out, his dream was prescient.

I was too small to excel at football, too short to play basketball, and I was quick but not a winning sprinter. My dad still wanted me to try many different sports, though, since my adult size was still to be determined.

He told me things like, "If you want something badly enough, you'll have to give it everything you've got." Also, "Do you know why kids in the ghettos will often become exceptional at what they do? Because they're hungry for success. They will practice, practice, practice."

Often, he would say I was spending too much time doing lapidary work in which I had developed a keen interest on. He told me I should be outdoors, practicing sports to develop the skill.

Dad also gave me a chemistry set and a microscope at a young age. No electric train though. Oh no. That was wasting my time watching a train go round and round instead of developing a skill.

When I was in sixth grade in Kansas City, I went out for Little League baseball and was terrible at batting. So my dad softened up a baseball and began throwing me pitches behind the house every day for a long time until I finally got it and started hitting the hell out of the ball. I became the star hitter for the Little League team that summer. The value of practice became internalized at that point. I had experienced success with it—just "practice, practice, practice."

This achievement orientation spilled over into music (my dad's nightmare), specifically drums. Gene Krupa was my idol.

Academically, I struggled. Concentration was a real problem. Daydreaming was constant so that I wouldn't hear much in class and couldn't read more than a sentence or paragraph before I would then lapse into daydreaming, having to read the same paragraph over and over again. The exceptions were in science and math, where actively solving problems would keep my attention. Understanding something was much easier than memorizing something boring. I still wonder how I managed to pass history, civics, social studies, and literature during junior high and high school.

Around my junior year in high school, I envisioned owning a nightclub and playing drums in my own jazz combo. I researched some information on restaurant schools. One day though, my chemistry and physics teacher asked me what I was planning for college. I told him I was thinking of majoring in music. He told me people major in music because they can't do anything else and that he didn't think it would be right for me.

I think because of this short conversation, I began changing my idea about becoming a professional jazz drummer in my own nightclub. A college major that would give me a career to fall back on, in case I couldn't succeed as a jazz drummer, seemed more reasonable. Thus, I enrolled in a pharmacy school at the University of Iowa.

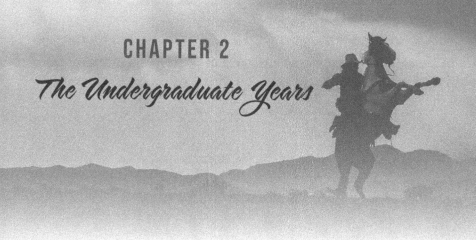

CHAPTER 2
The Undergraduate Years

*E*nrolling in pharmacy school was a good decision. The curriculum was chemistry, physics, and math, so my daydreaming was not as bad.

I studied very hard and excelled academically. In fact, one day, while walking to the library to study during my freshman year, I noticed the leaves were gone from the trees. Fall had come and gone without my realizing it. Now that's hyper focus.

Two sentinel events occurred over the next two years that were life altering. First, I got married at nineteen years old due to getting someone pregnant. This was a bad mistake I would later deeply regret. I had prioritized my career, so was not a good father. Later, other difficulties with my wife and kids would lead to a tragic outcome. Since it's not consistent with the theme of this book, to talk about these specific difficulties, let me just say that this early marriage made a "root hog or die" attitude necessary for me to accomplish my goals. In this sense, mentioning this early marriage is consistent with the theme of the book.

The second sentinel event occurred during my third year of college.

I read a book entitled *Atlas Shrugged* by Ayn Rand. I was blown away! The book gave me an understanding of the dichotomy between the oft-maligned self-interest and selflessness. The book championed and gave sanction to a rational self-interest, which, in my context, was focusing on personal growth and achievement rather than, for example, joining the Peace Corps at that point or carrying bedpans in Biafra. The book gave me confidence and comfort, knowing that doggedly pursuing a career had moral sanction behind it in a rational sense. I needed the certainty of knowing that being selfish in this context was good, not bad or immoral. Any guilt I had vaguely felt just melted away.

Another understanding I gained from *Atlas Shrugged* was an epistemological truth: humans must use reason to properly understand our world. This faculty of reason is strictly within the province of the individual since no collective brain exists in the real world. Only individual brains exist, and since reason is by choice and not automatic, then the responsibility of using reason exists within the individual. One can either choose to reason out an issue or choose to evade the issue.

The book also reasoned that self-ownership gives the individual the right and responsibility to controlling yourself and your choices. Thus, self-ownership and self-control became exalted values of mine. The desire to be my own boss came from these insights and would remain for the rest of my life.

Another important insight came from the study of philosophy over the next several years: contradictions don't exist in reality but can exist in our minds. This principle of noncontradiction would mean to me later that a physician's interests and his patient's interests are one and the same if the interests were rational. If the reasoning were correct and there still appeared to be opposing interests, then both the doctor and the patient should check the premises of their reasoning.

Academically, my undergraduate years were exceptional. I graduated magna cum laude with a BS in pharmacy. I had decided that, before graduation, I really wasn't interested in the practice of pharmacy. I was not an entrepreneur. My high school dream of becoming a professional jazz drummer had also cooled down. I loved the field of science and also wanted to be free from being an employee and become my own boss eventually. I decided to apply to a medical school with my exemplary academic credentials.

CHAPTER 3
Applying to Medical School

I applied to the University of Iowa medical school during my last year of pharmacy school. An interview was standard, routine protocol for students applying to medical school, and mine was scheduled with a staff microbiologist. Can you believe I failed the interview! I was granted another interview with a urologist. I passed that interview, but since I was fifty-fifty on the interviews (one was standard), I was required for an interview again, this time with a dermatologist. After that interview, I still had another interview, this time with a psychiatrist, who reported that I wasn't crazy! Clearly, somebody didn't like me.

I endured a total of six interviews, the last being with the dean of the medical school. He informed me that I had split the interviewers down the middle. Thus, he stated that since I had become a cause célèbre in that medical school, he didn't think it was wise for me to become a student there.

What on earth had I said that had caused such controversy? First of all, I was naïve, believing that institutions of higher learning were open to intellectual diversity even fifty years ago. (Be careful young people.) Secondly, when asked the standard question on why I wanted to become a doctor, I should have stated the selfless standard that I wanted to sacrifice my life to serving others. Ayn Rand had dispelled that attitude as a primary motivator several years before. The primary reason I stated was my love of science and that I wanted to become my own boss someday. That I would productively provide valuable service to patients was a laudable result, not as a personal sacrifice but as a personal achievement. I probably even stated at some point that a rational self-interest was proper to humans. So half the interviewers thought I was a selfish money-grubber and the other half thought, bravo!

Basically, I was turned down for my Randian understanding of ethics. Problem: in an interview, you don't have time to explain the rationale of these ethics, so they were misunderstood by half of the interviewers. Interestingly, the medical school stopped the requirement of student interviews the following year.

Being rejected from entrance into the University of Iowa medical school allowed me to complete a year of pharmacy internship in Illinois and to become a resident of that state. Then I could take advantage of in-state tuition and work my way through medical school as a part-time registered pharmacist.

That year of my pharmacy internship in Illinois, I applied for the state medical school and the Northwestern University medical school in Chicago. I was accepted to both schools, and neither school required an interview. I chose the more prestigious private school, Northwestern.

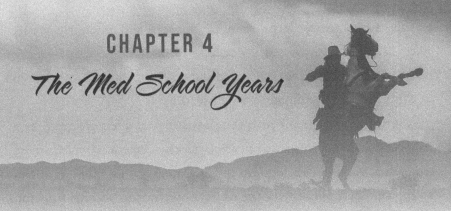

CHAPTER 4
The Med School Years

I was dreading the first class of the freshman year: gross anatomy. I'd never even seen a dead person, let alone slice and dice one. I wasn't looking forward to entering a lab full of human cadavers.

As it turned out, this class was the most important of all in two respects. First of all, the subject matter was all new to me, even the nomenclature, but was essential to master. Secondly, and most importantly, the process of intellectualization took place. All the squeamishness dissolved when I realized how much I had to learn in a relatively short time. There literally was no time for squeamishness.

Fortunately, this detached state of mind would become ingrained throughout most of my career. Otherwise, the pain and suffering of patients would not be just problems to be solved but could soon become emotionally intolerable for a doctor, leading to a shortened career, drug abuse, or even suicide. I became a scientist through and through.

One day, my dissecting partners and I were called into another cadaver lab to see something "interesting." The class was dissecting the genitalia at the time. What was interesting was a massive penis on this cadaver. It was larger than I'd ever seen and, of course, wasn't erect. Seeing this, I crossed my arms over my groin and announced that I was afraid I'd not yet entered puberty! This served to brighten an otherwise somber mood in the dissecting lab.

During my freshman year, the class attended a lecture given by a tall, slender, distinguished-appearing African American man, who I remember was a doctor high up in Cook County hospital. He began asking members of the audience why they wanted to become a doctor. The responses were routinely altruistic until I raised my hand and stated that my reason was I liked applied science and problem solving and I wanted to be my own boss. He chuckled and said, "Oh, you'll have plenty of bosses."

In my career that followed, I did have plenty of wannabe bosses, but they ultimately failed to control this cowboy.

I did well in the first two years of medical school and was the first 5 percent of students in my class of 1974 inducted into the Alpha Omega Alpha Honor Medical Society. The next 5 percent would be inducted after the next year.

While in medical school, I worked part-time as a relief pharmacist around Chicagoland. This helped pay the private school tuition, which in the early 1970s was $3,000/year (now twenty times higher at $60,000/year) and helped with family expenses.

The third year of school was the most stressful year of my life, no exaggeration. I had never examined a patient and applying what I had learned the first two didactic years to an actual patient was difficult for me.

The class was divided up so one quarter of the class would be rotating through one of four specialties: pediatrics, surgery, internal medicine, and obstetrics and gynecology.

My first rotation was in pediatrics. I knew nothing about how to integrate the findings on the history and physical exam of a patient and synthesizing it to a list of possible diagnoses (called the differential diagnosis).

A staff pediatrician would take a group of students to make rounds on the patients in the hospital. He would then pick one of us out and ask multiple questions about the patient and the diagnosis. I was mortified! I felt so incompetent, not knowing much of anything, so I tried to hide in the background, so he wouldn't notice me and call upon me.

The first day of rounds made my anxiety worse. He called upon a student to list the five signs of rheumatic fever (caused by a strep infection, usually strep throat). The student correctly stated, "Arthritis, carditis, chorea, subcutaneous nodules, and erythema marginatum." I about puked! How could the student have known this? I could feel myself flush even though I hadn't been called upon. Oh Lord, how long must I suffer?

During this third year, the only time I looked forward to was lunchtime. I couldn't wait for lunch. It was ecstasy! Then came more rounds.

Interestingly, even though the teaching method of being put on the spot in front of your colleagues was nasty, fifty years later, I have never forgotten a correct answer to a question asked of me or one of my fellow students using this approach.

Toward the end of this third year, things started to click, and my anxiety lessened significantly. However, the last rotation of my third year was internal medicine. It was mostly supervised by a resident doctor rather than a full-fledged staff doctor. I didn't seem to impress the resident, who was from Brooklyn, New York. Try as I might, I couldn't please him. On the last day of the rotation, he was especially being a jerk, and I exploded at the nurse's station. He and I had loud words, and he told me he was going to flunk me. I told him to go straight to hell.

Fortunately, there were many witnesses to the altercation. He did flunk me, but I scored extremely high on the final exam and had decent evaluations by staff doctors, so the resident flunking evaluation was thrown out due to personality conflict. That time right won; he lost.

The fourth year of clinical rotations was elective and less stressful. I was going to apply for a pathology residency, but my uncle, who was a professor of animal physiology at Iowa State University, knew I was wanting to go back to a rural area and mentioned I might not like pulling bodies out of ditches after long winters when they became exposed. Plus, my pathology advisor at Northwestern told me the field was becoming progressively more regulated, and I might not like it. He seemed to sense my libertarian independence, so I switched to applying for a general surgery residency.

My general surgery advisor at Northwestern wanted me to enter a prestigious "pyramid" surgery program, either at Duke University or the University of Michigan. A pyramid is where only a few of the residents starting the program finish the program.

I had already had my fill of intense stress during the third year and was sure the stress would return in this type of pyramid program. Since my home state was in Iowa, I enrolled at the University of Iowa for a residency in general surgery. It had been about six years since my awful interviews there, so I didn't think anyone would hold that against me since I had done so well in medical school.

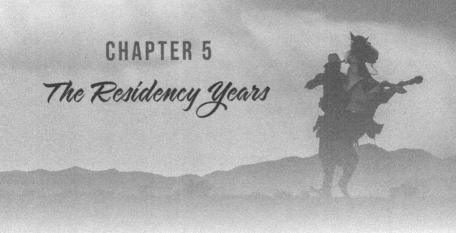

CHAPTER 5
The Residency Years

I spent only the first two years of five at the University of Iowa's Department of General Surgery.

The first year, called the surgery internship year, was grueling. Time spent on the hospital wards starting IVs, inserting various tubes into body orifices, participating in surgeries while holding retractors for hours, as well as studying amounted to about 100–120 hours per week. Plus, night call added even more hours. Meals again became the high point of each day.

Very little operating experience occurred during this first year except to hold retractors for exposure of intra-abdominal organs. This could be exhausting, especially on the bariatric (obesity) surgical rotation where a patient could weight up to five-hundred-plus pounds.

As an intern in surgery, I began to covet the anesthesia residents since they were given coffee and lunch breaks; whereas, surgery residents were required to stay for the entire case, sometimes lasting up to four-to-six-plus hours. One of the surgery interns switched to an anesthesia residency. I didn't want to wimp out, so I stayed in the general surgery program.

I continued at the University of Iowa for the second year of residency, even though two of my good friends left the program for Scott and White Hospital in Temple, Texas. One switched to a urology residency, and the other switched to an orthopedic residency.

It became clear that, if I stayed at the Iowa program, I would not be guaranteed operative experience until the fourth year, and even then, the experience could be reduced if you rotated on neurosurgery, burns, or gynecology.

Actually, the University of Iowa was more the rule rather than the exception in the northern states where didactic learning took precedence over operative experience. In the southern states, like Texas, operative experience took precedence. Their philosophy was that, as a surgeon in-training, you had to operate every bit as much as an athlete had to practice their sport and a musician had to practice his instrument.

I felt like I needed operative experience more than didactic learning. My residency friends, who had switched programs to Scott and White Hospital in Temple, Texas, gave glowing reports about the general surgery program there.

Thus, after the second year, I left the University of Iowa program for Scott and White Hospital in Temple.

I operated constantly at Scott and White, especially at the veterans' hospital. I either did the operation with the instructor as the first assistant or vice versa. I was behind the other residents in surgical skills since I had done very little operating at the University of Iowa.

After spending about a year there, I began to catch up. I started doing major vascular and thoracic cases at the veterans' hospital, and by the fifth year of residency, I had done about fifty stomach surgeries for peptic ulcer disease. This allowed me to help interns and first-year residents with these cases. I like teaching a lot and would miss it in private practice.

Interestingly, surgical skills and technics differed a lot among seasoned staff surgeons. Some surgeons were slashers and burners, some were very efficient in their movements, and some were nervous Nellies, who would fret over every little bleeder, even capillary bleeding, and they would fret and second-guess themselves on each step of the operation. This would ultimately cause more bleeding and trouble than the more efficient surgeons. Watching different surgeons operate was extremely valuable.

I found that surgery was a process of constant decision-making. Ultimate success in the field appeared to depend more upon the confidence and courage of the surgeon than in knot tying and suturing skills. These skills could be learned by mostly anyone, nonphysicians included, with practice time and muscle memory.

The process of surgical decision-making was how deeply to cut, how vigorously to spread the tissues, whether to use scissors or fingers at a given point, which bleeders could be cauterized, sutured, clamped and tied, or ignored. If the decision was incorrect, then getting out of trouble efficiently were all keys to a successful operation.

One slasher-and-burner type at the University of Iowa was angry at the nursing staff for getting the case started a bit later than 0730 on the dot. He angrily slashed through the abdominal wall with his scalpel that he sliced through loops of underlying intestine. Bad move! This wasn't a demonstration of courage and confidence. This was fury combined with arrogance on display, pure and simple.

I have found, over the years, that largely because confidence and courage are so dominant in the surgical process, not all surgeons are equally competent. Some competence has to do with repetition on the types of operative cases. Doing similar cases over and over again improves competency, but unless underlying confidence and courage are present, a surgeon won't perform as well. These necessary attributes I believe are innate, at least after late childhood.

I found that another essential attribute of a first-rate surgeon is honesty. Evasion from factual input is an enemy of success. All facts, good or bad, pleasant or unpleasant must be the allies of the surgeon. There is no place for optimism or pessimism. It's just the facts, period.

I found this to be especially true when a complication would happen in the postoperative period. Evasion from unpleasant findings, such as a rapid pulse, fever, or generalized abdominal tenderness and rigidity, can get you on the golf course earlier or temporarily save your egotistical belief that a complication couldn't have occurred in your hands, but the evasion leads to delay, and delay can lead to the demise of the patient.

During my residency at Scott and White, I witnessed what to me was an obvious evasion. It involved a patient who had a postoperative leakage of the bowel contents from a sutured connection of the two ends of the bowel.

Making rounds on the patient after her surgery, I thought she appeared sick or toxic and had more abdominal tenderness than I would have expected, even with the fresh surgical incision. I thought the patient clearly had an acute abdomen, necessitating an emergency reoperation.

I notified the staff surgeon, who had performed the surgery. He came and examined the patient but, somehow, was too optimistic about what he was seeing. A delay occurred, and the case turned into a mess once the reoperation was finally done. Evasion can be deadly.

I found that a dangerous attribute in a surgeon is too much

arrogance. I define arrogance as having an unrealistic assessment of one's own effectiveness. It's like unearned confidence.

As an example, as an intern rotating at the veterans hospital at the University of Iowa, I was observing a staff surgeon helping his senior resident perform a colon removal for cancer. Both surgeons were fancy slasher-and-burner types, and you got the impression, watching them, that they might start twirling and flipping their instruments like rock and roll drummers. They were rushing through the surgery. One of them spied a "lymph node," suspicious for the spread of cancer. Quick as a wink, he clamped the lymph node and cut it out without further investigation or caution. This was their fancy operative style. Hurry up! Hurry up! Twirl them scissors!

Postoperatively, the patient died in shock. The lymph node was found to be a piece of pancreas. The patient died of a pancreatic abscess on autopsy.

With the above observations during residency, it became clear that more was necessary to be a first-rate surgeon than technical skills. An absolute commitment that all facts are allies and are not to be evaded, having confidence and courage to make decisions without constant second-guessing, and basically being a first-rate person were necessary to make a first-rate surgeon.

Beyond residency, over the years, I experienced that these essential attributes are not automatic or even permanent, especially when under pressure and when ego maintenance and saving face become more important in difficult and critical times. I'll illustrate this further when I discuss the private practice years.

CHAPTER 6
Starting Private Practice

*D*uring the fifth and last year of residency, I interviewed with a private group of surgeons at a small community in Texas. I decided I'd had enough of the heat though. It could be so intense in the summer that rapidly coasting downhill on a bicycle would feel like a blast furnace. Also, large insects, like scorpions and tarantulas, bothered me.

I also interviewed in Utah a residency friend who was looking for a place to practice urology. He was a Mormon and grew up in the area so fit right in. I, on the other hand, sensed that being non-Mormon put me at a disadvantage, plus many general practitioners were still doing bread-and-butter surgery, so I would be competition instead of someone to refer cases to. I discovered how it felt to be a minority—uncomfortable.

Thus, I decided to head back to my home state of Iowa and interview at a large hospital in northern Iowa. Lots of family and friends were there, so this provided some comfort in the otherwise stressful period of starting a practice about which I knew nothing.

I interviewed the hospital CEO first. He pointed out that there was a multispecialty group and about an equal number of single-specialty practices. The CEO recommended that I start a private practice outside of the multispecialty group since the general surgeon who serviced the private practitioners was elderly and about to retire.

I also interviewed several private doctors in town and in the surrounding communities. They were all cordial and welcoming though one of the busy practitioners in an outlying community asked me how much of my fee I would split with him if he referred a patient and assisted me in the surgery. He said that since he had to travel to assist me, he needed more money than what insurance would pay him. I let him know that my mentors and the American College of Surgeons considered fee splitting unethical. Their reasoning was that the choice of a surgeon would be based upon how much of his fee he would split and not upon his skill.

I later found out the region was notorious across Iowa for this and that 40 percent of the surgeon's fee was customarily split with the referring doctor. It was scandalous in that part of Iowa.

I made the decision never to split fees. I accepted the potential risk to my practice. As it turned out though, I think it was admired and probably helped my practice in the long run.

One of the general practitioners I interviewed offered to take me into his practice and teach me the business details of running a practice. He really wanted me to come to the community to help with the rivalry between the multispecialty group and the private practitioners.

Recruiting a private surgeon into the community would be a feather in his cap to the other private practitioners. Since medical school and residency taught nothing about the business of medicine, I took him up on his offer.

Rent was low, and this was valued by someone like me who had yet to do his first case in private practice.

My first case was on June 30, 1979. It was an eighty-year-old man who presented to the emergency room (ER) with peritonitis from a perforation of his colon caused by a weakened spot called a diverticulum.

The doctor who referred the patient to me also assisted me in surgery. The case went smoothly, and the assistant was impressed (whew!). He and his two partners began referring most of their patients to me for general surgery.

Word spread quickly among the independent practitioners, and my practice grew quickly. The doctor who had shared his office with me wanted to form a partnership.

I became uneasy though when the partnership required that I give 40 percent of my surgical fees to the partner plus share the office overhead. Thus, realizing this was the fee splitting for which the region was so well known, I rented my own office space after six months of practice and became a solo practitioner.

General surgery, at that time, was abdominal, breast, thyroid, chest, and vascular surgery.

About 50 percent of my practice was emergency surgery since, as a solo practitioner, I was on call 24/7 and was the eager new guy in town. Even the multispecialty group didn't mind since one of their surgeons, while on call, would slip off to Lake Okoboji. This was one and a half hours away, so he wasn't of much use in an emergency.

One day, the first case of a ruptured abdominal aortic aneurysm came into the ER. An aneurysm is a thinning out and ballooning out of an artery such that it finally ruptures like a balloon. He survived the surgery and was the first survivor the town had seen. Other surgeons had tried and failed.

The next nine ruptured aneurysm patients survived under my care as well. Then, I started losing a few. My reputation for vascular surgery grew, and I was referred more elective aneurysms and arterial bypasses for the lower extremities. I became the dialysis vascular access surgeon for the region as well. Needless to say, I got very busy, sometimes too busy, though I was young and eager at that point so I didn't mind. I became the busiest of the four general surgeons in town, the other three being with the multispecialty group.

Each successful surgery felt like a significant achievement, and this feeling would remain throughout the forty years of my practice. I deeply loved my career.

CHAPTER 7
Harrowing Experiences

Surgeons who practice for forty years have many experiences, both good and bad. One of my mentors, a cardiovascular surgeon at Scott and White, told me something I never forgot: "Good judgment comes from experience, and experience comes from bad judgment."

Most of the bad experiences I was able to learn from though not all. These bad experiences from which no learning occurred were like the car accident involving a professional driver who had driven for years. Then one day, out of nowhere, boom!

One such case involved an elderly man who presented to the ER with a ruptured abdominal aortic aneurysm (AAA). His vitals were unstable, and he arrived in shock, a condition where the vital organs are unable to receive enough oxygen to function. Resuscitation started in the ER with fluid and blood infusions.

On my way to the hospital, I gave orders on my car phone to get the operating room ready, so when I arrived, we could cut.

His abdomen was sterilized with antiseptic and drapes were quickly placed over the patient prior to giving the anesthetic since this can cause the collapse of blood pressure in these unstable patients.

Quickly, after anesthesia was started, a long incision was made into the abdomen. Blood was within the abdominal cavity, and a huge collection of blood was around the ruptured aneurysm. I quickly got control of the aorta, above and below the aneurysm, by clamping the aorta (the largest artery in the abdomen) with large, specialized arterial clamps. This stopped the bleeding.

Since the aneurysm was now excluded from the circulation by the clamps above and below it, I was able to cut the aneurysm open to start placing a Dacron graft inside the aneurysm and sew it to the aorta above and below. This would restore circulation to the legs.

Suddenly, the patient lost all blood pressure and heartbeat. In spite of having good resuscitation to a good blood pressure, and in spite of having stopped the hemorrhage, the shock had taken its toll, and the patient was pronounced dead.

In order for him to be embalmed, I sewed off the open ends of the aorta, so all the embalming fluid placed at the funeral home wouldn't just all go into the abdominal cavity. We then closed the abdomen, and it was time to inform the patient's family in the waiting room.

It is always difficult to tell the family of the death of a loved one, though the family had been warned of his grave condition just prior to the operation, and that he might not survive.

The family had been placed in a private consultation room. When I walked in, they appeared ready for the grim news since the operation hadn't taken long. They knew something was up.

I sat down with them and informed them that the patient had passed away even though the bleeding had been controlled. Like the majority of Midwestern families, especially farm families, they were pretty stoic and understanding.

Suddenly, the door flew open and a wide-eyed anesthetist said they needed me quickly in the operating room! I sensed big trouble. Upon entering the room, I saw the patient had a pulse and EKG tracing of the heartbeat. He had come back to life!

Now, I had to think. First, I had sewn off his aorta for embalming. Secondly, he was without vital signs for such a long time that his brain was likely irretrievably damaged. I reasoned that even if he could survive, his meaningful life was over. Thus, after discussing my thoughts with the anesthetist, I instructed her to stop the respirator and let nature do its work. It did in short order.

I went back to the consultation room and informed the family that he had indeed expired and that after a few signs of life. He was gone.

This was clearly not a learning experience. It was a terrible experience that, fortunately, I would never have to witness again.

Another case was an elderly man found to have a lung mass on a chest X-ray. It was highly suspicious for lung cancer. It would require removal of a portion of his left lung if the lymph node sampling beneath his sternum showed an absence of the spread of the cancer.

The lymph node sampling was normal, so a surgical incision was made into his left chest. I had hoped to be able to remove only the upper lobe of his lung, but I could feel the enlarged, hard lymph nodes all the way up to the root of his left lung. Thus, removal of the entire left lung was necessary to also remove these lymph nodes.

The operation went smoothly, and I was finally able to clamp off the main artery to the left lung at its root. I then removed the left lung from the chest. All I had left to do was sew the large vessel closed, so I could remove the clamp. Suddenly, the clamp slipped off the artery, and the entire left side of his chest cavity quickly filled with blood! I was able to use my hand to stop the hemorrhaging from the artery. I could not see to clamp for the artery since too much blood obscured my view. Even when the blood was suctioned from the chest cavity, when I removed my hand to re-clamp the artery, it would immediately fill again with half the cardiac output, so I still couldn't see to clamp the artery.

I was stuck between a rock and a hard place and felt a terrible rush of adrenaline such that my hands and arms began to shake. I knew the patient's death was imminent if I couldn't get control of this artery.

Thinking was difficult in this state of fight or flight, so I knew the most urgent issue was getting control of my emotions. I had no options if I was unable to think. So with my right hand blocking off the artery, I took time to relax and started to quietly discuss with my assistant the actions we had to take. He was to suction any further blood accumulation in the chest with two suction devices. Blood was being given for the blood the patient had already lost.

Finally, we were ready to try to gain control of the artery, which was short in length, so there was not much room to clamp it. The shaking had stopped, and I was able to fully focus. If the first attempt failed, it was back to square one and try again. Hopefully, the artery wouldn't be torn in the process. My right hand I would remove from the artery, which would be quickly clamped with the instrument in my left hand. I told my assistant on the count of three. One, two, three! I simultaneously removed my right hand and clamped the artery with the left. Success! Success! Now was the time for smiles from the crew. I began laughing believe it or not. A laugh of pure relief and joy.

Lesson learned: staying calm and focused is key. Or if you do get an adrenalin rush, recover your wits first. Don't try to work in a frightened state of mind and body.

Many other such difficulties occurred over my forty-year career.

You think you've seen every possible problem, then up pops a new one you haven't seen. Having to deal with these problems makes a better surgeon.

"Good judgment comes from experience. Experience comes from bad judgment."

CHAPTER 8
The Scrub Nurse

There is nothing more sought after by a surgeon than a talented scrub nurse. They are truly unsung heroes. Functional brilliance shines through. Academic brilliance is of little use. Their attributes are natural—you either have it or you don't. Their typical disposition is such that they let flare-ups and nasty temper tantrums from asshole surgeons roll off their backs like a warm shower. Their anticipation skills are keen. They can anticipate what instrument a surgeon needs before he even knows. They learn the steps of an operation quickly and are ready with the proper tools for each step. A few have a knack for seeing the problem a surgeon is having and coming up with a solution, which the surgeon might not be aware of, especially under pressure.

With all this natural talent, they are grossly underpaid due to a healthcare system that's so snarled up with a massive regulatory state and top-heavy administrations that it couldn't care less about the talent or worth of scrub nurses.

A recent scholarly study shows why scrub nurses are paid less than a living wage (see Clin.Orthop.Relate.Res. (2018) 476:1910–1919).

From 2005 to 2015, CEO salaries at major, nonprofit hospitals grew 93 percent, which is five times the salary of an orthopedic surgeon and twelve times the salary of a pediatrician. CEO salaries increased forty-four times that of a registered nurse! Also, the number of plain-clothed nonhealthcare workers escalated due to the increasing burden of massive regulations. Imagine where the lowly scrub nurse might be on this totem pole!

In Iowa, a large healthcare system called Unity Point has a board that meets in Des Moines periodically. One of its functions is determining CEO salaries in nonprofit hospitals. The board contracts with a business firm specializing in CEO salaries. Guess who gets to pick the business firm? The CEO. See any conflict of interest there?

Perhaps in a competitive and less regulated system, surgeons could reduce their administrative office personnel and hire good scrub nurses then pay them what they're really worth. That would be one solution. Allowing scrub nurses to freelance could be another solution. Good nurses could even choose the surgeons they like working with. As it is, they don't make a living wage.

When I started bariatric (obesity) surgery later in my career, I needed and got a committed team of talented nurses. The surgery was complex with a long learning curve, and the American Society for Metabolic and Bariatric Surgery recommended a committed team.

Something unexpected happened when I started with a committed team: I grew attached to them. I bantered with them, philosophized with them, gossiped with them, laughed with them, and sometimes commiserated with them.

A couple of times, I took the team to the Estes Park YMCA camp for a seminar. We all stayed in a cabin and cooked delicious breakfasts and suppers of beef stew with corn bread, roasts, chicken—all delicious up in the mountains. Lots of laughs and booze at night too.

The seminar was to experience the value of a support group in patients who have undergone bariatric surgery. Rapid physical changes occur in these patients, as well as mental changes having to do with personal relationships, self-concept, you name it. It all requires support big time.

This team was to experience the value of support needed to hike up a steep mountain at high altitude. Fortunately, it wasn't a long hike, just steep. The reward would be at the summit of the mountain where the entire Rocky Mountain National Park could be viewed. Magnificent!

One morning, the team started with me leading the way while I played my harmonica once in a while. I got way ahead of them since I was better acclimatized. One of the girls decided she just couldn't do it and wanted to turn around. She was tearful. The rest of the team though became her support and kept encouraging her to keep going up the mountain. It worked!

They all made it to the summit to experience its magnificence, both the summit and the support. A large picture still hangs in my home of all the team in our OR scrubs on top of Emerald Mountain. See why I got attached to them?

It was this esprit de corps that kept me in practice until seventy-three years of age. I was having one hell of a good time. Giving that up was really difficult.

CHAPTER 9
Competition and Character

I always knew that to be successful, you would have to compete. Competition keeps you on your toes. It galvanizes you to be better today than you were yesterday. Bottom line: To really succeed, you need to try to be better than your competitors. Competition is a turbocharger.

That said, competition is not always comfortable. Many people try like hell to avoid it, or they'll try to create an uneven playing field to their advantage. Some will make competition illegal, calling potential competitors a duplication of services hence illegal, as we'll see later. Or many will cheat in other ways, sort of like stashing a card up their sleeve during a high-stakes poker game.

Benefits come from competition only if it's fair competition on an even playing field. This happens only when the competitors are of solid character or when honest referees are present. I experienced that in the field of medical care. The competition combined with poor character and/or biased referees can literally lead to the death of patients, even lead to something close to murder, as we'll see.

I knew up front when I started practice in the community, that competition was fierce between the multispecialty clinic and the independent doctors.

One of the reasons why fee splitting was so common in this part of Iowa was due to intense competition. Those doctors with less of the three As (availability, affability, and ability) could offer to split fees with doctors who referred a patient to them. This was officially considered unethical practice according to the American College of Surgeons, and a surgeon could be expelled from the college if proven. This seldom happened though hence the widespread fee splitting.

Perhaps another reason for the fee splitting in this community was because the business model of the multispecialty clinic allowed it since they were a business entity. It was considered ethical. Basically, the primary care doctors, like general practitioners and internal medicine specialists, would refer patients to the surgeons within their group. A portion of the surgical fees were put into a big pot and shared with the nonsurgical referring doctors. They could refer patients out of the multispecialty clinic, but there was no financial incentive to do this.

One time, a patient of a general practitioner in the clinic referred herself to me to remove her gallbladder. After the surgery was done, she went back to her general practitioner, who told her, "You knocked my teeth in when you went over to Dr. Ver Steeg." The patient told me about this on a follow-up appointment. I knew this doctor, and he was getting older, so I wrote him a letter about what the patient had told me he'd said about knocking his teeth in. I told him I knew a good dentist. "His name is Dr. Retirement." He shortly, thereafter, was investigated by the Iowa Board of Medical Examiners for multiple women claiming he had abused them. He quickly retired.

The competition between the multispecialty clinic and the independents remained intense during the first ten years or so of my practice. I found that surgeons with less talent gravitated toward multispecialty groups in smaller communities since referrals were guaranteed and a good reputation was not essential to be busy like it was in private, independent practice.

One evening, while I was in the emergency room, I found out a clinic surgeon who was on call was tending to a patient, who had a ruptured aneurysm in his abdomen. The patient was extremely unstable and was in shock from hemorrhaging despite the rapid fluid and blood infusions. Though he was on call, the clinic surgeon had been stopped from doing vascular cases like this due to poor outcomes and requirements of massive blood transfusions even during elective vascular cases.

I asked the ER staff if they could use my vascular expertise since they knew I did lots of ruptured aneurysms, usually with good results. They said the patient was being transferred by ground ambulance to Des Moines, a ninety-mile distance. Again, the patient had been in shock for too long in our ER, and the clinic surgeon tending to him was unable to perform the required surgery. He knew I was always on call for emergencies such as this and knew I was in the ER. He saw me there. In spite of this, the patient was sent by ambulance in profound shock to Des Moines, and as sure as the sun rises in the east, he died en route.

The next morning, the clinic surgeon and I were alone in the surgery dressing room. I point-blank asked him why he didn't refer the patient to me, so at least he would have had a chance of survival. The surgeon grabbed my shirt collar and put me up against a locker. Calmly but with seething anger he said, "Would you refer me anything you couldn't do?"

All in all, I couldn't believe what I had just witnessed. First of all, he had sent the patient out in an unstable condition to a certain death, which now would be illegal under current law. Secondly, it was too outrageous a decision to consider it malpractice—it was, at the very least, manslaughter. Thirdly, he gave me an indication that he was truly a monster that the combination of competition and weak character had made him become.

Without strongly ingrained character traits, like honesty and concern for your fellowmen, all bets are off when you are under the pressure of a dire emergency and competition.

I notified the Iowa Board of Medical Examiners about the incident. I should have notified the police instead. As it turned out, one of the clinic surgeon's referring clinic doctors, a recovered drug addict, was on the board of the Medical Examiners. Thus, the verdict was that it was his word against mine. Even though the death incident spoke for itself, this was the outcome due to biased referees.

To reiterate, competition in healthcare is necessary, but the participants must be of good, strong characters. Otherwise, it can result in a tragedy.

CHAPTER 10

The Golden Years of Medical Practice

I began private practice in surgery in June 1979. Office practice was straightforward then, in that very little red tape was required.

Patients were given a "superbill" after an office call or surgery. The patient would send the superbill into their insurance company, and the amount would be sent to the patient in the form of a check. The patient would then pay the doctor's office for the amount owed.

The doctor wrote the reason for the office call on a six-by-four-inch card, including pertinent history and physical findings, and a plan. Usually, a paragraph or two would suffice. If the patient had been referred by another doctor, then that referring doctor was sent a letter and sometimes a phone call. If the patient was scheduled for surgery at the hospital, then the history and physical was dictated on the hospital line and transcribed. At least one doctor in town would handwrite his history and physical and send it to the hospital.

Healthcare delivery was straightforward and simple with minimal paperwork and overhead expense. I got by with just one employee. In short order, I added a receptionist.

This golden age of healthcare delivery lasted until circa 1984. Then, the system planners started in. Managed care insurance companies started to become dominant, ostensibly to help control healthcare costs. Doctors' fees were frozen by Medicare for the next eight years.

My hospital tore out bathrooms and treatment rooms where doctors could perform minor procedures without an emergency room charge for inpatients. All these rooms were remodeled into offices for plain-clothed nonhealthcare workers charged with managing the length of hospital stays, as well as managing the escalating number of regulations heaped upon them by Medicare, Medicaid, and managed care insurance companies. This was all in the name of cutting costs. Watchdogs were created such as the Iowa Foundation for Medical Care (IFMC) to decide the length of hospital stays for a given illness and to improve the quality of care.

One of the general practitioners admitted too many patients for tests since insurance companies wouldn't pay for tests done, unless the patient was hospitalized. He would also keep them in the hospital too long. It was true that he was guilty of doing this. Thus, the IFMC came to the rescue and put all doctors on the staff, not only the offending doctor, on probation. We all had to call the IFMC for permission to admit and even discharge patients to the hospital. These were long phone calls with no reimbursement for our time, only the IFMC's time. This was just a hint of what was to happen over the next several years to reduce healthcare costs and improve "quality."

Early on, when this onslaught of regulations began, I knew higher costs were ahead, not lower costs. I made some coffee cups with the words, "Ration Health Bureaucracy, Not Healthcare!" I knew instinctively the former would lead to the latter.

I was given a stern warning by a reviewer for the IFMC because I performed a hernia repair on a man as an outpatient. I sent him home before he took a crap! You might wonder how a surgeon, who vowed to be his own boss, would tolerate this atrocious letter. I burned it!

I often wondered what sort of swamp creature would give up a practice to become a reviewer or head an organization like the IFMC. I found out in only a few years—one of the top heads of the IFMC was convicted of tax evasion, and the other one lost his license due to substance abuse. Yes, sir, the golden years of medical practice was officially over for us and those two swamp creatures.

CHAPTER 11
Massive Bureaucracy and Vested Interests

*D*uring this transfer of authority for patient care from the practicing physician to oversight organizations, insurance companies, and other system planners—such as politicians and their favored academics—costs for providing medical care soared and continued to soar, just the opposite result promised by our politicians and academics.

Some might think the massive escalation of costs is due to the magnificent technological advances we've all witnessed in the last thirty years or so. Actually, technological advances, though initially high in cost, lead to dramatic declines in cost if free competition is present. For example, the first quartz watch, called an Accutron watch, was priced at about $140 in the early 1960s. This was an expensive watch in those days. Now, they are free with a box of Cracker Jacks. The same has been true for most all technology unless it involves the healthcare system. Nearly everyone can now afford a handheld smartphone with a computer more powerful than those that helped us land on the moon.

The key has been competition in our free markets. The healthcare system though has actually succeeded in outlawing competition through prohibitive regulations. You don't have to be a rocket scientist to predict what would happen to pricing.

The Certificate of Need (CON) laws came about in the mid-1960s, starting in New York and then gained traction to become a federal law in 1972 under Nixon. The competition was judged by the liberal, left-leaning academics and politicians to be a duplication of services, so outlawing or limiting competition would help lower healthcare costs, according to these illustrious brains.

These laws basically required that to start competing with an existing healthcare entity, such as a "nonprofit" hospital, the proposed new competing entity had to demonstrate a need and not just be a duplication of services. This was to be decided by a CON board run by the state government.

Guess what? The boards became dominated by nonprofit hospital administrators. If a doctor wanted to build an endoscopy lab, for example, he would be defeated by the CON board.

Preventing competition in healthcare through regulatory laws has caused healthcare cost to soar, in addition to the costs of the regulatory burden on the system. Plus, Nixon also signed the HMO Act of 1973, which started another massive regulatory snarl-up by our insurance companies.

The cost of complying with these "cost-reducing" regulations became enormous, which included costs to doctors' offices. I refused to equip my office with electronic medical records. I was docked 2 percent of my Medicare fees, but 2 percent of 40 percent of the usual fee that Medicare paid was a pittance compared to the cost of the software I would have needed to purchase. Plus, electronic medical records had been installed in hospitals, and doctors used them to greatly increase their fees for daily hospital visits by having the computer spit out the past—family history, social history, full medication list, etc. This would increase the level of the visit to a level 5, for example, instead of a level 2, which was all that was usually necessary for a daily visit with the patient. Healthcare costs increased, but hospitals love it since their doctors were employed and the hospital could increase their revenue and, hence, administrator's salaries.

Doctors that placed this software in their offices were angry because it cut down on their efficiency by about 50 percent. Many had to stay late at night to get the records into the computers, so they hired scribes to do this for them. Are you beginning to see a problem here? How did all this lead to lower healthcare costs? It didn't, and it wasn't supposed to lower costs. It satisfied the vested interests of software companies and the egos of the system planners. It's just too obvious with the massive escalation of healthcare costs that cost reduction wasn't really their motive. Now that the system had become so complex, hospital administrators' salaries skyrocketed as discussed in chapter 8. The push toward a "Medicare for All" system was undoubtedly the motive of socialist-leaning politicians.

CHAPTER 12
Cowboy Doctor

*I*f you look closely at these cost-saving laws and regulations, you will notice they all have one thing in common: to stifle competition. Most doctors don't want competition, and hospitals wanted to outlaw it, or at least create a severely uneven playing field. Here's how they did it.

When I started practice in 1979, there was about an equal number of independent, single-specialty practices, and a multispecialty clinic. The competition was manageable; and even more important, the playing field was even.

An even playing field was present largely because hospitals were prohibited from employing doctors. The reasoning behind this was because nonprofit hospitals didn't pay taxes and were able to have tax-free foundations, so doctors employed by them would have great financial advantages over their private practice counterparts. Hospitals could contract with doctors for services, like pathology and radiology, but not actually employ them.

In circa early 1990s, this changed though through a legal sleight of hand. Nonprofit hospitals began to use tax-advantaged foundation money donated charitably to them in order to purchase doctors' practices in the entire region and employ them. They even fired some doctors if they took too long with patients, even good, competent doctors.

Hospitals around the state began vying for regional market share by buying up practices in surrounding counties.

This could be lucrative for those doctors whose practices were bought, especially those about to retire. If a doctor wanted to remain independent, then the tax-advantaged money was not available to that practice.

This didn't affect my practice or patient load until the hospital purchased the multispecialty practice and took the practices in all the surrounding counties and combined them with the multispecialty clinic. They were all placed under one clinic name.

Being a general surgeon, this essentially cut off my referral base. The effect wasn't immediate since I had a good reputation and some loyal referring doctors. Over a few years though, it started eating into my practice.

One fine day, a colleague drew my attention to a local newspaper article where the physician head of the newly formed hospital group was interviewed. The doctor was asked if there were any doctors left in the region that were not part of the giant group. He said, "Oh, there are a few cowboys left out there."

I thought to myself, "Hmm? I've always admired cowboys. If any single type of individual represents metaphorically the traditional American values, then it's the cowboy." Independence, self-reliance, competence, and courage represent American cultural values and reside in the spirit of the cowboy.

I bought myself some cowboy boots, cowboy shirts, slim jeans, a couple of Western belt buckles and a Stetson hat. I wore them around town, in the office, and the hospital. I would wear a white coat once in a while, but in the office, patients relaxed more after seeing the cowboy attire rather than the white coat.

I was going to remain an independent doctor come hell or high water regardless of less income.

I helped form the North Central Iowa Physicians Association, which championed independent practice. It really didn't build up much steam though since many of the independents were slowly deciding their interests, and safety would be with the hospital doctors. There were still several of us cowboys who stayed in private practice.

CHAPTER 13
Scrambling to Find a Niche

I started looking into other areas of practice not dependent upon physician referrals. I also began employing my wife, Phyllis, in order to cut overhead costs.

The first area I investigated was cosmetic vein surgery. This was accomplished with lasers, injections, and minimal skin incisions to treat spider veins and varicose veins on the lower extremities. Several trips for seminars were required to learn these procedures.

This was only of minimal help to my practice since spider veins were not a big concern to rural Iowans, plus I would spend too much time on these procedures for what I could charge since cosmetic surgery wasn't covered by insurance.

I expanded into laser hair removal and tattoo removal, and again, I found rural Iowans weren't into cosmetic surgery so much. Plus, the laser cost $80,000 to purchase.

One day, a man came to the office, wanting to remove all his body hair, so he could transition into a woman. This took many sessions, and he began to run out of money. I continued anyway, and he would pay whenever and whatever he could. Unfortunately, the laser finally broke down, and it cost me $10,000 to get it repaired. It became clear I wasn't going to come out ahead with lasers, so I gave the laser away and stopped with the nonsense.

Then I got a phone call from my son who was enrolled at Northwestern University medical school. He said he observed complex stomach surgeries being done laparoscopically for severe obesity. With laparoscopy, no large, painful incisions were made into the abdomen. Only little pokes into the abdomen were made where narrow tubes were inserted, then instruments were able to be passed through these tubes, including a television mini camera. The surgeon would then watch the television monitor to see himself performing the operation.

I didn't believe it at first, but then found an ad for a surgery meeting at Mount Sinai Hospital in New York City where live video demonstrations of the surgery could be viewed, as well as a didactic portion of the meeting.

My wife and office manager, Phyllis, and I flew to New York to the meeting. Not only could I hardly believe what I was seeing, but I was hooked! Not only mastering this surgery would be a big achievement, Iowa was rife with severely obese people, and this type of surgery would allow me to jump over the hospital multispecialty clinic referral base and enhance my practice. I even advertised in the newspaper and radio, "No referral necessary."

I also knew that one of my competitors was a poor technician and wouldn't be capable of learning the procedure. The other surgeon was too busy with everything else, so I wouldn't have a problem getting an adequate volume of cases to learn the procedure and maintain proficiency.

I flew to Orange County, California, with Phyllis. We spent a week there. I observed laparoscopic gastric bypasses with a certified mentor for the American Society for Bariatric Surgery (ASBS), Dr. Milton Owens, and also made hospital rounds with him and saw patients in his office. Phyllis spent a week in the office, learning all about running a bariatric office and its many pathways with Tina Napora, Dr. Owens's office manager.

The week was intense. Dr. Owens was an efficient surgeon and a very good mentor. Plus, he had boundless energy. He would work from sun up to sun down and into the night, doing paperwork or even writing scientific papers. With all this, he would find time to lift weights with a trainer then eat and have a couple of martinis. He was in his midsixties. Following him around made me exhausted by the end of the week. Phyllis was so stressed out; she broke out in shingles on Venice Beach at the end of our week. I laugh now, but it wasn't funny at the time.

The following week we spent in Las Vegas, taking a didactic Essentials course with the ASBS followed by a test that was required to pass the course.

In August 2002, I performed my first gastric bypass. The first ten surgeries I did through an open incision in the abdomen, using the same instruments I would be using laparoscopically through the ports (tubes) rather than making an incision. I practiced suturing and knot tying in a cardboard box with holes punched in it to simulate laparoscopy. Bananas and oranges were used for the objects to be sutured.

Before starting to do laparoscopy for such a complex procedure, I flew back to New York with my surgical assistant at laparoscopy. We spent another week at Mount Sinai, observing three bariatric surgeons. I had plenty of questions before I would start such a complex procedure laparoscopically.

As a humorous aside, Phyllis and I were to meet my surgical assistant and his wife in the Rainbow Room at the Rockefeller Center for dinner the first evening. They didn't show up for a while, so we thought maybe the quickie lasted a bit longer than expected. Finally, they came through the door, and my assistant had this suit jacket on that hung to his knees and the shoulders were wide enough for an NFL linebacker! My assistant was a small guy, about five foot five inches and 120 pounds dripping wet. So he was allowed into the Rainbow Room wearing the only extra jacket they had hence the delay. Rural Iowa attire is very casual.

We finally performed the first laparoscopic gastric bypass toward the end of 2002. I was nervous, as was my assistant, but all went well though slowly. It took us about four and a half hours.

The year 2003 was my busiest year for bariatric surgeries of all the seventeen years that I did it. We performed 177 cases, mostly laparoscopic. Then the regulations started pouring in. The ASBS required a minimum of 125 cases per year to be an ASBS certified Bariatric Center of Excellence (COE). The ASBS then successfully lobbied Medicare to only allow Medicare patients that included the disabled to be done in COEs. Private employers in my town and elsewhere, as well as insurance companies, stopped coverage of bariatric surgery or required a six- to twelve-month diet supervised by a physician. These new regulations made the 125 cases per year requirements difficult to reach in a rural area.

I looked at Mercy Hospital in Mason City and Iowa Methodist Hospital in Des Moines to see if I could combine my region with one of those regions in order to get the caseload required to become a COE.

The Mason City Clinic was independent from the hospital and was a beautiful facility but required that I take general surgery and trauma calls in addition to all bariatric calls and keeping my original office practice open. This was not acceptable, so I declined.

Des Moines didn't require trauma or general surgery call, but the practice was hospital-based and the instruments I needed were declined by the hospital. So I declined them also.

Thus, I was stuck to grow my original bariatric practice while taking trauma and general surgery call. We also gave patient seminars and frequent support groups to satisfy the requirements in order to become a COE.

I still was barely making the volume requirements when, out of the blue, my bariatric mentor, Dr. Owens, called me and asked if I was interested in joining a bariatric surgery group he was forming in California, where each surgeon would be located in a different community to create a wide region in Southern California.

We flew out to interview Dr. Owens and the Lancaster Community Hospital in Lancaster, California, where I would be setting up practice. Phyllis and I were excited about it since Lancaster Palmdale were sister communities with a combined population of about five hundred thousand, and no other bariatric surgeons were in the area.

California or bust! When we arrived in Lancaster, we had been promised a turnkey program with an office, and instruments I would need in surgery would be ordered and available. All we needed to do was get there as soon as possible and start seeing patients.

When we arrived, nothing had been built for the office. It was more or less an empty shell without cupboards, desks, or flooring. The program coordinator was hostile to Phyllis right off the bat. We were angry that the things promised were not done, and everyone was angry. What a welcoming atmosphere! I also found out the administrator at the Lancaster hospital had not signed the agreement with the bariatric surgery group yet.

What a doofus I was. Bear in mind, I was not a businessman and had never moved a practice before. I was basically a little lamb about to be feasted upon by sneaky entrepreneurial wolves.

In Iowa, one's word or a handshake was as good as gold, so I trusted people to a fault.

In spite of the rocky start, I managed to get three surgeries on the schedule. The instruments were supposed to be available. On the eve of surgery, the instruments were not there, so I canceled the cases. The hospital administrator, being such a sweetheart exploded, when he heard I canceled the cases. I also became ballistic.

An emergency meeting was scheduled the following morning with the sweetheart administrator, the business manager for Dr. Owens's bariatric surgery group, and Phyllis and me. By the way, the business manager had not yet seen to it that the hospital sign the contract. This started to stink real bad! The hospital administrator and the practice manager were real friendly with each other though.

The key question I asked was, with all the time they had to order the instruments I required, why weren't they available? The administrator the day earlier said they were held up in a snowstorm. That day he states, "Well, I thought a wrench was a wrench."

That was the last straw. He clearly had no respect for surgeons probably due to his own incompetence and, hence, jealousy toward those who are effective. Whatever. I was done.

We packed up our things in a U-Haul with some hired help and moved back to my original practice in Iowa. We lasted a total of six weeks in Lancaster. God, it felt good to be back.

Unfortunately, we couldn't find a liability insurance for six months due to their reticence to insure bariatric surgery, which was considered legally high risk. Finally, the bariatric society (ASBS) started their own insurance product.

Even though I still had hospital privileges in my original community, they gave up my office space. I had to remodel a filling station into a doctor's office. This took some time.

This was a very expensive and difficult odyssey for Phyllis and me. I did learn a lot about identifying and trusting "slickmeisters" though. Either watch them carefully or better yet, don't mess with them. Overall, business people don't have the same ethical standards as most physicians. Again, "Good judgment comes from experience, and experience comes from bad judgment."

CHAPTER 14
The Cowboy Rides Again

*C*irca May 2005, I was back in my original practice. Fortunately, my loyal referral base was still there as were the bariatric patients. I continued taking calls 24/7 to improve my caseload. Phyllis continued as my nurse and business manager, and my original employees were glad to be back.

We restarted the bariatric program, and it took off well since I had established a good reputation in the region.

I sensed the multispecialty hospital group wasn't too happy with my return, and I became concerned they might try recruiting a bariatric surgeon for the hospital. So I had an agreement drawn up that if they agreed not to recruit a new bariatric surgeon while I was in town, I would agree to learn no new laparoscopic general surgery procedures. The hospital surgeons, the hospital CEO, and I all signed the agreement.

This worked out well for a while. I was performing enough bariatric surgeries to maintain competence, and my competitors didn't worry I would compete for other advanced general surgery cases by learning to do them laparoscopically.

Over the next year, I became busy enough with bariatrics that I decided to recruit a bariatric surgeon myself. Plus, I was close to sixty years of age and 24/7 call was starting to be a bit much.

Thus, I informed the hospital recruitment office of my desire to recruit another bariatric surgeon for my practice. They had helped other independent practices with recruitment before, and they agreed to help. It would mean more surgeries and more revenue for the hospital.

In fairly short order, they located a possible recruit. I was thrilled! The surgeon was a woman finishing up her laparoscopic fellowship and agreed to interview with me.

The date was set for the interview and site visit. I inquired about the time she would arrive, so I could meet with her, show her around, and get to know her. They informed me I would have one hour with her. The rest of the time, she would be interviewing and having lunch and dinner with the hospital clinic. What a swindle! So much for the Iowa handshake being good as gold. They were stealing my potential recruit!

I did get the chance to inform her that the multispecialty hospital group, the hospital CEO, and I had signed a noncompete agreement for bariatric surgery. I said I would love to have her join me in practice and that the bariatric program should be under one roof. I also said the hospital had supposedly been recruiting for my practice.

She and I got along well, but she became wary of the rift between the hospital clinic and the independent doctors. She decided not to come.

I wrote a letter to the hospital board, including a copy of the agreement we all had signed. An attorney on the board wrote back and said the agreement was not legally binding.

Cute! I hired an attorney in Waterloo, Iowa, specializing in hospital-physician issues. His opinion was the agreement was legally binding since there was the required quid pro quo.

My attorney sent a letter to the board, stating the agreement was enforceable and that they should "govern themselves accordingly." I received a reply from the hospital attorney stating I must immediately stop this "tortious" behavior.

My practice continued as before, but things felt tense. Then one afternoon, out of the blue, I got a phone call from Mercy hospital in Mason City. The doctor on the phone was head of the Mercy weight loss center and wondered if I'd consider setting up practice in Mason City to become the bariatric surgeon for the weight loss program. They were willing to come to my office for a meeting. With the crap happening in my hospital, I could hardly believe the potential opportunity.

The meeting went well. They wanted me to start a bariatric surgery program in Mason City, and we agreed that I could continue my bariatric office as before at their expense, but that all surgeries would be done in Mason City.

This was my chance to combine the two regions of Iowa and then get enough cases for my long sought-after center of excellence. This would increase the caseload further since Medicare would then allow me to perform surgery on Medicare patients as a COE. I would train a surgeon, who had an interest in bariatrics, in Mason City. Since there would be two bariatric surgeons in Mason City, I would only have to take half the call once the surgeon was trained, and I would be offered a guaranteed income until the program was established. Since Mason City was ninety miles away and a thirty-minute response time was necessary when on call, I would purchase a place to live in Mason City and keep my home here as well.

I was to be employed by the independent Mason City Clinic and "leased" by the hospital. No general surgery of trauma call was required.

Wow! I couldn't pass it up. Now was my chance to become an ASMBS designated center of excellence by combining the two regions of Iowa for the required case members. Only my original hospital would be the loser. Since I would have a presence in the town and my reputation of twenty-five years was good, it was unlikely the hospital clinic would be able or even want to recruit a bariatric surgeon. Few surgeons were willing to take 24/7 call.

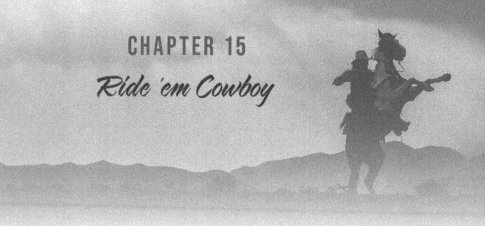

CHAPTER 15
Ride 'em Cowboy

I started seeing patients in Mason City in October 2008. I already had about one hundred cases pending from my original practice, so things started off with a bang.

Phyllis, my wife, was under contract with the Mercy Bariatric Clinic to teach the nursing staff about the pathways required for a certified bariatric program. We started in the same office together with the nurse, but someone decided Phyllis and I had to be weaned from one another. This was my first inkling that I was losing control of things. She was placed in another office where I would have no physical presence.

A program coordinator, who was pleasant and friendly with everyone, was hired, and she and Phyllis quickly became good friends. Unfortunately, she became overwhelmed with the scope of the work required of her, so she quit the weight loss center and was transferred to another hospital position.

Another coordinator was quickly hired, being transferred from another department into the weight loss center.

This coordinator proved to be bad news. She would play people like she was playing a pipe organ with a certain theme, and people were like the stops on the organ being pushed and pulled that was consistent with the leitmotif.

In the context of the bariatric program, the leitmotif was getting Phyllis terminated. I informed the clinic managers in the hierarchy that, if this happened before the end of Phyllis's contract, I would also leave. One of the managers said that, regarding setting up a bariatric surgery program, "We don't know enough about it to know what we don't know." That also included the new coordinator. Thus, since Phyllis had run a bariatric program single-handedly for six years, they had her stay longer.

The stops continued to be pushed and pulled by the coordinator though, and this was when I realized I had no control over what was happening. I even went to the hospital administration to complain, but they took the coordinator's word for everything. She was higher in the corporate hierarchy, so they didn't believe a word I said. The administrator, who dealt with hospital staff—physician conflicts, told me it was reported that I was creating a hostile environment and needed conflict resolution classes.

It became clear to me that when I was my own boss, everything went smoothly. I had gone into medicine to be my own boss. When I was in a corporate structure with hierarchy, I couldn't tolerate what I perceived as the abusive, sneaky personality types who tended to do well in the corporate structure and would gravitate to higher positions in the hierarchy.

This gave me the choice of either accepting others with less knowledge, expertise, and competence to be my boss or not accepting it and getting out from under the corporate model.

Phyllis's contract was terminated a few months later though she was told she could apply as an insurance clerk. Of course, this was at the bottom of the hierarchy. She left the job, so I terminated the "lease" agreement with the hospital and left the Mason City Clinic and set up my own office in Mason City off-campus.

I continued the bariatric program at Mercy hospital in Mason City and my original office in my original place of practice. We were now a center of excellence.

My partner, whom I had trained, left Iowa and became a transplant surgeon in Tampa, Florida. Thus, I took all bariatric calls except for seven days per month. Four of those days, I saw patients in the original office.

We hired a nurse in Mason City, who also acted as our receptionist and a bariatric exercise coach at the YMCA. She was well known in the Mason City community and had been a nurse at Mercy hospital for years. She had also had bariatric surgery by my previous partner.

She was initially nervous about coming into our practice, but after a few weeks, she told Phyllis that what she had been told about us was clearly wrong, and that we were nice folks to work with. She informed us that when she was a bariatric patient, the coordinator had told her, "She would rather die before she would let Dr. Ver Steeg do surgery on her."

Finally, I had the proof I needed to get the coordinator fired! The patient (now my employee) wrote a letter to the hospital administration, telling them what the coordinator had said to her. I also called them. The patient said in her letter she would "go head to head" with the coordinator if she denied it.

The coordinator was immediately fired from the bariatric program. Finally, someone believed me in the administration. Another coordinator was hired, and we got along very well for the rest of the time I practiced. The program also continued to thrive. Everyone was happy until a new bariatric surgeon came to town.

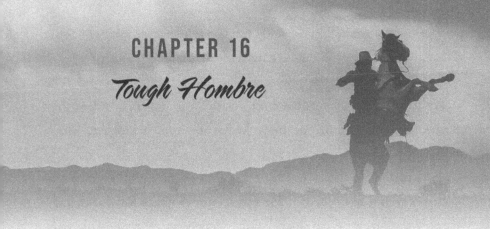

CHAPTER 16
Tough Hombre

The newly recruited bariatric surgeon was a poor technician. He required an average of four and a half hours to perform a gastric bypass. Every step of the operation required multiple looks—second, third, and fourth looks. A more difficult case could take all day, even into the night. These cases, as a comparison, would take the previous surgeon or me about one and a half hours more or less.

As I discussed in an earlier chapter, the process of surgery was about making multiple, quick decisions. Dexterity could be learned by most without difficulty. His technical skills, such as suturing and tying knots, were adequate. His downfall was his decision-making.

From day one, he was very unfriendly to me and wouldn't cover my postoperative patients very well. He acted like an unfriendly competitor who wished I had left Mason City when I left the Mason City Clinic. He was now employed by them, along with his being leased by the hospital. He thought I shouldn't be there.

Reports from a few of my patients said that, on my weekends off, he would peer into the patient's room, not bother to examine the patient, and at least once told the patient that he would not have done the surgery the way I had done it. This he said even though he wasn't present at the surgery. Now, that gave the patients a strong sense of security!

The hospital, since they were paying his salary, favored him. The Mercy weight loss center sent him a lot of the patients, unless they specifically requested me, or unless he became too backlogged, which was usually the case.

Fortunately, at the end of his five-year contract, the hospital told him they would not renew it. He was a big monetary loss for them. I was only revenue for them since, being independent, they didn't have to pay me a salary except for call pay. I would now be back on call for all but seven days per month, four of those to see patients in the original community office.

CHAPTER 17
Some Rough Riding

*C*omplications could arise in patients undergoing bariatric surgery regardless of the experience and skill of the surgeon. One such complication was bleeding from the connection made between the miniaturized stomach and the intestine in gastric bypass surgery. This connection is done with a stapler with suture reinforcements. This was finally solved by using a patch made from a bovine heart sack, called a pericardial patch. This would be sandwiched into the connection. Once we started using this patch, bleeding became rare.

Another type of complication was a leak from this same connection. It happened infrequently, but when it did, it could be terrible. Great pain, shock, sepsis, and reoperation would result. I would notice when reoperating, that the entire connection would unzip and come apart. I couldn't figure out a way to prevent this devastating problem until the pericardial patches were back ordered for several months. This turned out to be serendipity. We had to contact another company with a similar patch, but it was synthetic and not made from a bovine heart sack. The company representative came with the alternate type of patch and gave us very competent instructions on its use.

In the representative's presence, we began using his company's synthetic patch. He showed us data on how the thickness of the synthetic patch was 0.4 mm in thickness without variance. The pericardial patch though varied from 0.4 mm to 1.2 mm in thickness. I immediately reasoned that since the staple length was not variable, the thicker patches would cause the staples to become too short and not seat correctly. A cardiac surgeon also informed me that the pericardial patches would sometimes calcify in some areas, possibly causing the staples to not penetrate.

We canceled the back-ordered pericardial patches and started using the synthetic patches exclusively, and to my knowledge, the problem of leaks was solved.

CHAPTER 18
Chasing a Costly Mirage

As it turned out, my goal of achieving a center of excellence status became nothing but a mirage. The ASBS decided to drop the volume requirements to fifty cases per year instead of the 125 requirements. Also, Medicare decided they would no longer require a designated center of excellence to perform that surgery on their patients.

This blew me away! I had traveled to California to achieve COE status without success and moved to Mason City to also become a COE. Now, at a cost of well over $1 million, it was all unnecessary. I was chasing a regulatory scheme created by crony capitalists (lobbyists) that could be changed upon a whim, and it was. I could have stayed in my original practice though the uneven playing field there was nasty too.

I was able to learn from this expensive, disruptive experience though. Don't chase government regulations. They're an ephemeral mirage, and even worse, the persons responsible for the regulatory schemes and those who are enablers don't give a rat's ass about the harm it reaps on an individual.

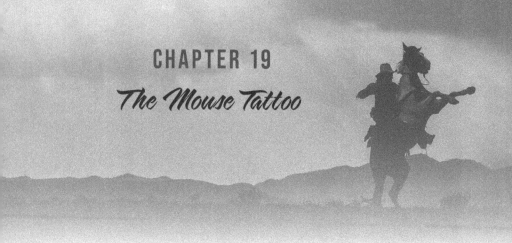

CHAPTER 19
The Mouse Tattoo

I worked several years after the last surgeon had left, and everyone had a great time in the operating room. The OR team was well-oiled, and we all could relax, listening to music, having conversations about love, life, children, and cracking jokes. What a wonderful time to be alive!

I had several cigar parties with the OR staff and their significant others. During one party, one of my scrub nurses said she had a tattoo of a mouse on her upper thigh near her groin and asked me if I would like to see it.

"Yeah," I said, "let's see it."

She pulled down one side of her underpants, so I could see the mouse tattoo. I couldn't see it. Instead of pulling her pants down farther, she said, "Oh, my pussy must have eaten it!" Only in rural Iowa.

Then one morning, in the operating room, we were doing a case. The usual crew was there, including the scrub nurse with the mouse tattoo. A young, pretty student nurse observing the case was standing behind me. I was preoccupied with doing the surgery, but the team was bantering back and forth, so I started thinking about the mouse tattoo. As a joke I was going to ask the scrub nurse to show me her mouse tattoo. I addressed her and said, "Show me your pussy!" God, did that come out wrong! The student nurse flushed red, and the room roared. All I did was shake my head at the faux pas. To this day, I have never lived that down.

Only in rural Iowa!

CHAPTER 20
Cronyism and Payback

I wasn't the only cowboy in my community. There were several independents that didn't join the hospital clinic, but they just didn't dress like cowboys. Several of them left the hospital as I did.

A group of orthopedists had left the hospital multispecialty group because of revenue sharing with lower income primary care (legalized fee splitting though still unethical in my view).

The orthopedists joined forces with an independent cowboy orthopedist and developed a hugely successful practice as the only orthopedists in the area.

The multispecialty hospital group was not happy about this. It prevented them from successfully hiring an orthopedist for their own group to continue the fee splitting.

The orthopedists lost a partner due to cancer, so only three of them were left.

They requested the hospital to allow one of their physician assistants (PA) to take first call for the ER once or twice per week. Plus, they requested hospital reimbursement for their ER coverage since this was the growing trend nationally and in Iowa.

The hospital CEO and clinic were like peas in a pod. The executive committee was dominated by clinic doctors, so together with the blessing of the CEO, they had the pleasure of denying the orthopedists' requests for the call issues. Thus, the orthopedists resigned from the hospital staff. Since they were independent, they didn't have to honor a noncompete agreement.

This became a huge financial blow to the hospital because, like me, the orthopedists didn't move out of the area but set up an orthopedic and sports medicine clinic in the community. They also obtained hospital privileges at a local hospital only forty miles away and continued a thriving orthopedic practice for the entire region.

The hospital and the hospital clinic tried to recruit an orthopedist or two, but they eventually left due to the intense competition from a superior orthopedic group. Eventually, my original community hospital was left without any significant orthopedic coverage. This was a multimillion-dollar blow each year to the hospital, plus my resignation from the hospital cost them several million dollars per year. Over the next ten years, they had to cut their beds to less than half of what they had during the heydays.

The cronies had been determined to crush the cowboys but lost the battle big time in the end.

You know what I think the sweetest victory was? The orthopedists operated at a small town hospital, and the high school football team's name was the Cowboys!

CHAPTER 21
And the Cowboy Rides Away

*U*nfortunately, after forty years of practice, the infirmities of age started catching up with me. The Mason City Clinic had hired another bariatric surgeon who was excellent this time. We got along great and taught each other new ways of skinning the cat though he had more to offer than I did, even though he was young and had only practiced for about ten years or so. Plus, I was set in my ways and hated to change a technique since there were always unintended consequences in changing something. Plus, "If it ain't broke, don't fix it."

I knew retirement was near. I had worked with the new surgeon for about a year and had informed him early on that I would spend about two more years working. It was only about a year.

I set the date and informed my partner and the hospital. I agreed to take call for about six months to give them time to recruit another surgeon. Phyllis asked if I wanted a retirement party, and I told her, "Absolutely not." Plus, she knew I didn't like surprises.

A few months after I had retired, Phyllis and I were going to attend a fiftieth wedding anniversary party for her brother and sister-in-law. It was held at the Community Orchard at the edge of town, which is a beautiful, bucolic setting her brother and sister-in-law had created. It was like a wonderland for children and adults.

We arrived and were walking on the sidewalk when I saw that a mural had been staked up in the ground. It was a picture of a cowboy on a horse, riding off into a beautiful sunset. On the mural were words that said, "As George Strait sang, 'And the cowboy rides away.' Have a happy retirement." I thought that was nice for them to recognize me at their fiftieth wedding anniversary.

All of a sudden, I see scores of these familiar faces cheering and smiling at me! Wait a minute. This is no anniversary party. I can't explain the cascade and mixture of emotions I suddenly experienced. Fear, happiness, embarrassment at being surprised, amusement, and warmth at seeing my two teams that had been with me day after day for so many years in so many good times and so many rough and tough cases.

I didn't feel sadness at that point, only later, while I was giving an impromptu talk on the stage where the band had been playing. The speaking was pretty easy until the end when I said, "You know why I continued practicing until I was seventy-three years old?" Suddenly, I felt an overwhelming sadness and such gratitude that I had to stop speaking for a while, as I struggled with emotions. Finally, once I was sure I had composure, I said, "It was the camaraderie I felt with my team in the operating room. I had a hell of a time giving that up." Kicking my cowboy boot in the air, I said, "All the rest of my experience with healthcare was shit!"

And the cowboy rode away.

EPILOGUE

The cowboy is the quintessential American. Born into freedom, he is the metaphorical avatar of independence, self-reliance, competence, and courage.

The cowboy doesn't want or need someone centrally planning his life. These systems planners have always been wrong about everything. Healthcare is the prime example of this, as are the one hundred million deaths caused by socialist experiments in the twentieth century (R.J. Rummel, Democide vs. Other Causes of Death, [February 1, 2005]).

Not everyone wants the risks of cowboy independence. Some prefer institutionalized practice, and that should be their choice as Americans. Cowboys will always, and should always be, with us though. Attempts to thwart them through regulations that stifle competition (CON laws) or create uneven playing fields is clearly flawed thinking.

To this cowboy, the unalienable rights of life, liberty, and the pursuit of happiness means the right to take all the actions necessary for our life and its enhancement. These rights are derived from our nature as animals with a volitional, rational faculty, and these rights are indeed natural law and are inviolate.

So to all the regulators, competition haters, central planners, and their chosen politicians, Don't tread on me. I'll fight as will all Americans who still know the value of freedom.

The End